Praise for **Naked Before God: The R**
by Bill Williams with Martha S. Willia

. . . . .

"Bill Williams' *Naked Before God: ⊥ne Return of a Broken Disciple* is an extraordinarily successful work of true narrative theology. He creates and sustains a fictional reality of uncommon depth and imaginative power even while offering a nuanced Christian apologetic. I have been as deeply moved by this book as by anything I have ever read. If life permits you to buy and to read only one book in a year, or in three years, or seven—let this be the one."
—*Catherine Wallace, author of* Dance Lessons

"What Williams knew is this: God is good. Life is really hard. How he knows this, and helps us to see Christ crucified, risen and redeeming in it is the stuff of a book I wish every Christian could read."
—*Reviewed by Barbara Cawthorne Crafton in* Episcopal Life

"Seldom does one have an opportunity to see the marriage of modern living to apostolic times with the application of the Gospel in as clear and perfect design as in the person of a First and Twentieth Century Nathaniel. This Lutheran theologian performs a great service in interpreting the Gospel in terms that the lay person can well understand and a challenge to deeper study in the exercise of faith and practice. No church library should be without it."
—The Counselor *newsletter*

"Never before have I read a book of theology that I could not put down. Writing with utter honesty and passion, in the face of his own death, expressing his doubts openly, Williams still searches for meaning."
—*David Rhoads, Professor of New Testament*
  The Lutheran School of Theology at Chicago

"Nathaniel is the disciple of Jesus who fled naked from Gethsemane in the early first century. He is also living on borrowed time from both diabetes and cystic fibrosis in the late 20th century. This is his journal and this is how gospel can still be done."
—*John Dominic Crossan, author of* The Historical Jesus

Manna in the Wilderness
A Harvest of Hope

Manna in the Wilderness
A Harvest of Hope

Meditations by Bill Williams
Illustrations by Martha S. Williams

MOREHOUSE PUBLISHING
HARRISBURG, PA

Morehouse Publishing
P.O. Box 1321
Harrisburg, PA 17105

Morehouse Publishing is a division of The Morehouse Group.

Printed in the United States of America

Cover design by Corey Kent

Cover illustration—hand-painted silk scarf by Martha S. Williams

Library of Congress Cataloging-in-Publication Data

Williams, Bill 1960–1998
     Manna in the wilderness : a harvest of hope / meditations by Bill
Williams ; illustrations by Martha Williams.
          p.   cm.
     Includes bibliographical references.
     ISBN 0-8192-1782-4 (paper)
     1. Bible—Meditations. I. Title.
BS491.5.W54 1999
242—dc21   98–55924
                                                                CIP

Contents

This work is dedicated to
the people of Calvary Lutheran Church
in Clarkston, Michigan;
the people of Lebanon Lutheran Church
in Hegewisch, Illinois;
the Students, Faculty, and Staff of the Lutheran School
of Theology in Chicago;
and to
Joan Swander,
who wrote us a sermon.

Has anyone told you?
You are all ravens.

• • • • •

Grateful acknowledgement is given to
Warren Geier and Joan Swander, who contributed their
talents to the original work.

• • • • •

Special thanks are due to Bob Walters and Bob Klonowski,
who shepherded me through the journey.

• • • • •

Thanks be to God for Martha Williams,
who illustrated, proofed, criticized, advised, loved,
and faithfully walked every mile that led to this book.

Cloud of Hope

Take a 4-foot strip of masking tape and crumple it into a little ball. Don't make it neat; let it be wild and woolly-shaped. Make sure the adhesive sticks out in spots.

Take it into your bedroom.

Roll it under your bed.

If you keep house like I do, it'll come out the other side with all sorts of fluff, cat hair, and pretzel crumbs attached to it. In fact, it may become so clogged with debris that it won't roll at all. It may not even make it out the other side.

That's the way I feel, sometimes. I seem to accumulate mistakes, missed moments, and past sins just like that ball accumulates cat hair. Everything sticks to me.

Families are like that, too. Hurts and misunderstandings pile up. People can get so clogged up that they can't roll straight anymore: their paths get crooked. They start to do real evil to each other. Then they have kids, and their kids have kids… and after a few generations, you end up with people who can't roll at all.

Nations can be like that, too. Whole societies can become overrun by their own history. Every group is aggrieved, every contract broken, every dream deferred: the nation grinds to a halt, halfway under the bed.

Who cleans house?

Who gets rid of the cat hair?

To start like water
Poured anew from fresh cotton
A sky-blue cloud of hope
Rebirth
Is not some cheap trick
But the intent of all creation
The clouds cleanse
What mud has made
Sully and sore and weary of earth
You will be clean again
You will be like rain upon the sea
Free from stain
And all the wrong
You thought you never would escape
The cloud, that cloud
That holy cloud
That cloud will bring you change
    —And so, of course,
        You fear the cloud.

The paradox of our desires:

      We want to improve,
    but we don't want to change.

I'm addicted to my captivity. I trade predictability for liberation. I cling to my prisons. I may resent what keeps me captive, but, when push comes to shove, I have to admit that I prefer my misery to an uncertain future.

As folks used to say: "Take the devil you know over the

devil you don't know."

After all, if you try to change things, it might get worse.

Trapped by the paradox of our desires, most of us act as if it's enough to simply wish for a better life. "I'll pray about it" becomes a cop-out phrase, yielding to the impossibility of our conflicting desires. We hand the problem off to God, saying "Here, you figure it out—"

"—Save my marriage, but let me behave the same…"

"—Make my work more interesting, but don't make me try anything new…"

"—Make me healthy, but let me keep the same habits…"

How does change break in on such a hopeless picture?

I think it's a gift.

I think the very same force that created the universe remains hovering on the outside edge of what's barely possible, luring us forward, pulling us toward a greater vision of what can exist. I think that's what creation means. It's not a one-time event, but a process that goes on and on, always enticing us to walk toward a world that makes sense.

That's really what the Genesis creation story is all about, after all: it's a simple story about a God who comes upon chaos and starts to clean things up.

"You there, Light, pull away from that darkness."

"You Waters, get together. Let's see a little dry land…"

Countless years later, there's still quite a bit of chaos lying around to clean up.

"You there, the one with the rotten marriage…"

"You there, Mr. Bigshot with the 200K salary…"

"You there, the wreck with the bottle…"

The finger points at us, and we experience a wild moment of clarity. All our powers of denial break down. We can no longer ignore the dismal condition of our lives. In a burst of honesty, we put together the two sentences that are the prerequisite for change:

"This stinks."

and

"I don't have to accept it."

Those are two sentences worth praying for. When we rub those two sentences together, sparks fly. A crazy, inspired moment passes when anything—even happiness—seems possible, and we cannot play it safe anymore.

Those are the moments of miracle, the Passover suppers of our lives. Like the nation of Israel in the book of Exodus, we act just a little nuts. We bake bread without leaven, eat freedom, spread blood over the door, and put our travelling shoes on. We stop saying "Yes sir" to the people and things that hurt us. We stop acting like slaves. We stop being slaves.

We become something far more dangerous: responsible people armed with hope.

Listen
A rumble, freedom
Like a storm in my stomach
This bread calls me
From the nervous dark
Waiting
Dangerous to eat
I swallow it and you are close
I know, I know
I've failed to change
Familiar manacles on my soul...
Oh, I know
I have these chains
I thought, it seemed
I mean—

They won't let go,
Unless I turn this key...

Oh Death, Slave Trader
Mocker, you Sin

I cannot stop this
Crazy rush
I think
I know
I will be free
I have to do it
I have to move
That's what I heard
The bread say and
I have to do
What the
Bread
Says.

God also spoke to Moses and said to him: "I am the LORD...
I have also heard the groaning of the Israelites whom the
Egyptians are holding as slaves, and I have remembered my
covenant. Say therefore to the Israelites, 'I am the LORD, and
I will free you from the burdens of the Egyptians and deliver
you from slavery to them. I will redeem you with an out-
stretched arm and with mighty acts of judgment. I will take
you as my people, and I will be your God. You shall know that
I am the LORD your God, who has freed you from the burdens
of the Egyptians. I will bring you into the land that I swore to
give to Abraham, Isaac, and Jacob; I will give it to you for a
possession. I am the LORD.'" Moses told this to the Israelites;
but they would not listen to Moses, because of their broken
spirit and their cruel slavery.

Exodus 6:2, 5–9

Parting the Red Sea was not Moses' greatest moment.
The real miracle was getting the Hebrew slaves to believe
in freedom.

Imagine an entire nation walking into the desert.

After that, everything else was just a footnote, a parlor
trick.

POSSIBILITY MATHEMATICS

1000 POSSIBILITIES:

AFTER ONE STEP TO THE RIGHT = 500 POSSIBILITIES

ONE STEP UP = 250

ONE STEP TO THE LEFT = 125

ONE UP = 62

TO THE RIGHT = 31

DOWN = 15

RIGHT = 7

DOWN = 3

LEFT = 1

The Tabernacle

Once we've decided to walk into the desert, we start worrying about which way to turn.

Oh, it's easy enough to find the desert, of course—but most of us are interested in getting back out again.

Sandra enters the Thursday-morning stillness of the church, quickly slipping past the lighted office and the shuffling sounds in the kitchen.

The pastor's parking slot is empty, so the hall past his study is safe to cross. The narthex, however, is broad and naked, peopled with imaginary border guards. She makes a furtive dash through the open space and steps, with relief, over the boundary of the sanctuary.

The air is hot and stifling. The fans are off.

She walks tentatively, counting the pews. Number thirteen is hers on Sunday, but today it looks hard and uninviting. The carpeted steps up to the altar would be far better.

She moves on into foreign territory.

This is where the
Burgess's sit. This is
the Kay's. This is the
lady that makes deli-
cious coffee cakes.
This is the grumpy
man that never says a
word.

This is no-man's land,
too close to the pulpit.

As she advances down
the aisle, she notices the
beauty of the stained glass
windows for the first time.
Normally the color of dull
cement, they glow with the
power of the sun, bestowing

rich blues

and deep dark purples,

forest greens,

blood reds.

She wonders why they don't turn
the lights off more often.

Maybe she should try the sunrise
service.

The altar looks unadorned, shrunken,
burglarized. She's disappointed. It is a
wooden table today, nothing more.
She didn't know that altars had the
day off.

Nevertheless, she has a hard time
stepping onto holy ground. She
stops at the first step and sits down.

She watches the altar. For what?
There's no life there.

The life is outside, pouring
through the windows.

She feels foolish.

Why is she sitting here in the
dark?

She thought she would
pray, but now it seems
silly, play-acting, stilted.

She is a modern woman,
struggling through the
other six days of the
week. Her problems
seem real and over-
bearing, while God
seems... unreal; from
another time.

Why are you here?
Because there's nowhere else to go.
Because I need a direction.
Because I thought you would help.
Why are you here?

In the distance, she hears a vacuum cleaner running, brr-rrr, across the carpet.

She smiles as she studies the organ pipes, which have been left as a decorative ornament. The new organ is electronic. It plays recordings of real organs which are still maintained somewhere in Germany.

The vacuum cleaner increases like an approaching storm. She sighs and gets up. She did not feel like talking to anyone today.

Why are you here?

The janitor, Ed, sees her and waves. She waves back. He nods and returns to his work.

She is grateful for his manner. Her embarrassment at getting caught eases. You would have thought it was perfectly natural for her to be sitting at the steps of the altar on a Thursday morning, the way he greeted her.

He is a quiet, good-humored man. His wife has something wrong with her. She saw something in the bulletin. Was it cancer?

Continuing to vacuum the carpet, Ed casually glides across the narthex, into the library.

It's not until he shuts the door, muffling the burr of the machine, that she realizes that she's been given a graceful, elegant gift. He is gone, but unobtrusively: No Big Deal.

Another few minutes in the dark to unwrap her gift, and then she rises and walks back into the outside world.

She has the same problems and questions she had entered with—but they
are colored differently.

They are

rich blues

deep purples

forest greens

blood reds...

and the soft,
neutral beige
of a Sears
Power-Vac
2000.

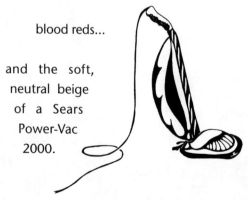

We long for well-drawn maps and itineraries, but all we get is an initial vector, and a plea to place our trust in smoke and mirrors.

On the day the tabernacle was set up, the cloud covered the tabernacle, the tent of the covenant; and from evening until morning it was over the tabernacle, having the appearance of fire. It was always so; the cloud covered it by day and the appearance of fire by night. Whenever the cloud lifted from over the tent, then the Israelites would set out; and in the place where the cloud settled down, there the Israelites would camp... As long as the cloud rested over the tabernacle, they would remain in camp. Even when the cloud continued over the tabernacle for many days, the Israelites would keep the charge of the LORD, and would not set out. Sometimes the cloud would remain a few days over the tabernacle, and according to the command of the LORD they would remain in camp... Sometimes the cloud would remain from evening until morning; and when the cloud lifted in the morning, they

would set out, or if it continued for a day and a night, when the cloud lifted they would set out. Whether it was two days, or a month, or a longer time, that the cloud continued over the tabernacle, resting upon it, the Israelites would remain in camp… but when it lifted they would set out. At the command of the LORD they would camp, and at the command of the LORD they would set out. They kept the charge of the LORD, at the command of the LORD by Moses.

Numbers 9:15–23

If you wait until it looks safe, you'll never go. The Spirit has to rush us out the door before we come to our senses and realize that we don't know where we're going. That's why Passover meals have to be eaten according to the chef's instructions:

This is how you shall eat it: your loins girded, your sandals on your feet, and your staff in your hand; and you shall eat it hurriedly.

Exodus 12:11

THE
MORNING
AFTER
FREEDOM'S PARTY
CRAWLING OUT
OF BED TO
HOT SANDS AND THE
GLARE OF A MORE
THREATENING
DAY;
YOU TRICKED ME
SLY SPIRIT
GOT ME DRUNK ON
POSSIBILITY
AND LURED ME OUT HERE
WHERE I'VE GOT NOTHING BUT YOU.
WHERE ARE THE LEEKS
AND ONIONS?

WHERE ARE THE FISH?

In Transit

Make no mistake about it: you will be punished if you try to change. We are a nation of databases and file cabinets, and we worship the Known Quantity. We're happiest when there's a slot for everyone, and everyone is in their slot.

Even if you're a disreputable sort, you will be less suspect than someone who's in transition. No one knows who you are or what to do with you; there's no written procedure for you; they'll have to talk to their superior; there's no funding for that sort of thing...

Why can't you just be happy in your slot?

Halfway detached
From a past that seemed
Oh-so-easily discarded
Only a moment ago
It wasn't just history
It was me
And I knew who I was
Back then
      I answered smoothly
      No stammer
      I was your slave, your junkie
      Your punching bag, your meat.
      I was an artist,

A preacher
A fireman, engineer
Mailman
Historian
Librarian, son.

Now I'm just
Between
Just between right now
Please excuse my dust
I cry under construction
And fall down a lot
Just between—
Is there a spot on this form
For just between?
Or when I go
Will you mark me down as

Unemployed

Nothing

Disabled

Has-been

Wash-out

Recovering alcoholic

Bad credit risk?

There's some pretty good, practical reasons folks don't go wandering out into the desert.

It turns out your basic instincts are right: change is not a picnic. It's a dirty, dangerous trek. It's going to hurt. You're going to run into plenty of demons and roadblocks.

To be completely honest, however, there are also plenty of angels, and their kind of roadblocks, waiting out there, too.

The trick lies in figuring out what kind of roadblock you've run into. I'm still trying to learn how to do that.

So Balaam got up in the morning, saddled his donkey, and went with the officials of Moab.

God's anger was kindled because he was going, and the angel of the LORD took his stand in the road... with a drawn sword in his hand; so the donkey turned off the road... and went into the field; and Balaam struck the donkey, to turn it back onto the road. Then the angel of the LORD stood in a narrow path between the vineyards, with a wall on either side. When the donkey saw the angel of the LORD, it scraped against the wall, and scraped Balaam's foot against the wall; so he struck it again. Then the angel of the LORD went ahead, and stood in a narrow place, where there was no way to turn either to the right or to the left. When the donkey saw the angel of the LORD, it lay down under Balaam; and Balaam's anger was kindled, and he struck the donkey with his staff. Then the LORD opened the mouth of the donkey, and it said to Balaam,

"What have I done to you, that you have struck me these three times?" Balaam said to the donkey, "Because you have made a fool of me! I wish I had a sword in my hand! I would kill you right now!" But the donkey said to Balaam, "Am I not your donkey, which you have ridden all your life to this day? Have I been in the habit of treating you this way?" And he said, "No."

Then the LORD opened the eyes of Balaam, and he saw the angel of the LORD standing in the road, with his drawn sword in his hand; and he bowed down, falling on his face. The angel of the LORD said to him, "Why have you struck your donkey these three times? I have come out as an adversary, because your way is perverse before me. The donkey saw me, and turned away from me these three times. If it had not turned away from me, surely just now I would have killed you and let it live." Then Balaam said to the angel of the LORD, "I have sinned, for I did not know that you were standing in the road to oppose me. Now therefore, if it is displeasing to you, I will return home." The angel of the LORD said to Balaam, "Go with the men; but speak only what I tell you to speak." So Balaam went on with the officials of Balak.

Numbers 22:21–35

I have friends who always assume that resistance to their plans comes from the devil. I'm not that confident, myself. When the road gets rough, I always start to wonder if it's because I'm heading the wrong way.

In fact, out of all the creatures waiting for me out there, the most confounding one is myself. When the path starts to narrow and break up, when my options tighten, that's when I meet myself out on the road—and the meeting usually isn't very pretty.

See, the dirty little secret is this: I'm not sure I deserve (or want) liberation. I cling to my brokenness like dog tags. When someone tries to set me free, my secret comes out. It turns out my support for the whole project is wafer thin: I'm just looking for evidence that the whole thing was a delusion, a bad idea cooked up in the heat of communion.

It turns out God has another jailer to worry about: Me.

ARE YOU LOST
YOU MAPLESS ONES
WHO CHASE RECEDING DREAMS?
DOES THE TRICKSTER SPIRIT
GLIDE IN FIFTH DIMENSION
HEEDLESS OF YOUR OWN TERRAIN?
IT PASSED THROUGH MOUNTAINS
YOU HAD TO CLIMB
AND PAUSED AT PUZZLING PLAINS
IT FLED THE PLEASANT MEADOW
DOUBLE-PACE, FRANTIC
    AND CAMPED FOR DAYS
    AT WILD ROCKS AND TUFTS OF SCRUB
WHICH YOU ATE, DESPERATE
    FOR FIGS.

Fever in a Forgotten Cave

There is a point in this story where everything breaks down. It doesn't matter who the story is about; the story is the same.

I'm not sure why it has to be that way. Maybe we carry the seeds of our own destruction inside of us.

I started out this story, remember, by talking about the paradox of our desires: how we want to improve our lives without change. Maybe that's the root of our tragedy. Maybe that's the seed of our destruction, the time bomb that's just waiting to go off.

Ultimately, we always discover that the Spirit of Restless, Permanent Change wants too much from us. We were looking for a little tinkering, and it wanted a major overhaul. We were talking about getting a tooth filled, and it was talking about ripping out our jaw, redesigning our bone.

At some point, our divergent interests always come out of hiding, and everything comes unglued.

Personally, I can't help but recall one of the worst weeks of my life, a pitiful time when I could do nothing but lie on the carpet of a motel room. I was delirious most of the time, unable to think of anything but the simple in-out, in-out of breathing. It was an animal existence, a time of shameful brokenness. All hope poured out of me like water.

Dreams died. Faith died.

Oh, I still knew that God was out there, I guess; but I stopped believing that would have any positive impact on my life. If anything, God seemed to be a malevolent force, punishing and cruel, taking me beyond the limits of my endurance.

When I was able to put together a coherent thought, it was to pray a sad, simple prayer:

Please kill me.
Let's end this.
This is not any fun anymore.
Let's not have anymore encores, okay?
I just want to go home now.
If you love me,
please kill me.

That's one of those prayers, obviously, that went unanswered at the time.

And that, of course, made me even angrier.

FAITH:

It's the ability to trust God, the sure knowledge that God wishes you well, no matter how bad things feel or look. It is, ultimately, a conviction that God is good, not evil.

Some people come naturally to that kind of conviction.

And the rest of us need miracles.

Now when the people complained in the hearing of the LORD about their misfortunes, the LORD heard it and his anger was kindled. Then the fire of the LORD burned against them, and consumed some outlying parts of the camp. But the people cried out to Moses; and Moses prayed to the LORD, and the fire abated. So that place was called Taberah, because the fire of the LORD burned against them.

The rabble among them had a strong craving; and the Israelites also wept again, and said, "If only we had meat to eat! We remember the fish we used to eat in Egypt for nothing, the cucumbers, the melons, the leeks, the onions, and the garlic; but now our strength is dried up, and there is nothing at all but this manna to look at."

Now the manna was like coriander seed, and its color was like the color of gum resin. The people went around and gathered it, ground it in mills or beat it in mortars, then boiled it in pots and made cakes of it; and the taste of it was like the taste of cakes baked with oil. When the dew fell on the camp in the night, the manna would fall with it.

Moses heard the people weeping throughout their families, all at the entrances of their tents. Then the LORD became very angry, and Moses was displeased. So Moses said to the LORD, "Why have you treated your servant so badly? Why have I not found favor in your sight, that you lay the burden of all this people on me? Did I conceive all this people? Did I give birth to them, that you should say to me, 'Carry them in your bosom, as a nurse carries a sucking child,' to the land that you promised on oath to their ancestors? Where am I to get meat to give to all this people? For they come weeping to me and say 'Give us meat to eat!' I am not able to carry all this people alone, for they are too heavy for me. If this is the way you are going to treat me, put me to death at once—if I have found favor in your sight—and do not let me see my misery."

Numbers 11:1–15

Yeah, there's a lot of weak-faith, struggling people in the Bible. Moses, Jacob, Elijah...

They all wondered, from time to time, just whose side God was on. Halfway through the journey, they all began to wonder if God really had their best interests in mind.

No matter how far they were willing to go, God always demanded just a little bit more; and they collapsed.

Ahab told Jezebel all that Elijah had done, and how he had killed all the prophets with a sword. Then Jezebel sent a messenger to Elijah, saying, "So may the gods do to me, and more also, if I do not make your life like the life of one of them by this time tomorrow." Then he was afraid; he got up and fled for his life, and came to Beer-sheba, which belongs to Judah; he left his servant there.

But he himself went a day's journey into the wilderness, and came and sat down under a solitary broom tree. He asked that he might die: "It is enough; now, O LORD, take away my life, for I am no better than my ancestors." Then he lay down under the broom tree and fell asleep. Suddenly an angel touched him and said to him, "Get up and eat." He looked, and there at his head was a cake baked on hot stones, and a jar of water. He ate and drank, and lay down again. The angel of the LORD came a second time, touched him, and said, "Get up and eat, otherwise the journey will be too much for you." He got up, and ate and drank; then he went in the strength of that food forty days and forty nights to Horeb the mount of God. At that place he came to a cave, and spent the night there.

Then the word of the LORD came to him, saying, "What are you doing here, Elijah?" He answered, "I have been very zealous for the LORD, the God of hosts; for the Israelites have forsaken your covenant, thrown down your altars, and killed your prophets with the sword. I alone am left, and they are seeking my life, to take it away."

He said, "Go out and stand on the mountain before the LORD, for the LORD is about to pass by." Now there was a great wind, so strong that it was splitting mountains and breaking rocks in pieces before the LORD, but the LORD was not in the wind; and after the wind an earthquake, but the LORD was not in the earthquake; and after the earthquake a fire, but the LORD was not in the fire; and after the fire a sound of sheer silence. When Elijah heard it, he wrapped his face in his mantle and went out and stood at the entrance of the cave. Then there came a voice to him that said, "What are you doing here, Elijah?"

1 Kings 19:1–13

This Empty Cup

The messengers returned to Jacob, saying, "We came to your brother Esau, and he is coming to meet you, and four hundred men are with him." Then Jacob was greatly afraid and distressed; and he divided the people that were with him, and the flocks and herds and camels, into two companies, thinking, "If Esau comes to the one company and destroys it, then the company that is left will escape."

... The same night he got up and took his two wives, his two maids, and his eleven children, and crossed the ford of the Jabbok. He took them and sent them across the stream, and likewise everything that he had. Jacob was left alone.

Genesis 32:6–8, 22–24a

The river bank is hard
     under Jacob's shoulder
    and the damp air has
       stiffened his joints
      which need to pop
       but won't.
    They persist, instead,
        in fiery discomfort
        neither here nor there
        Just like his life:
           inflamed tension
           poised at the river.

Oh, crack me
        end this long night
        either way, back or forth
        end this night, Lord.
They wrestle together
        his liberator, his
                demanding taskmaster,
                        cruel and unwilling
                                to hear no
and he, unwilling
        to say yes
        to more rivers,
                more crossings,
                more hard Jordans
                and more
                        sorrow words.

He has been a scoundrel
and he has cheated love
        always like this:
                good reasons for himself
                and ever-after regrets
                        always slipping away,
                                too many
                                clever days, and
                                        only the long night
                                                to claim him,
                                                only guilt at night.

I am sorry
but I can't go on

I have had enough
healing like this
You demand too much of me.

And I am sorry
but you haven't gone
far enough
Your wounds persist
because you won't
let me heal them.

You call this healing?
You call this help?
You call this peace?

You have to own
this pain before you
can give it to me.

He has sent all his loves away
        He thought it might be the price:
            Go on, go on,
                Without me!
        But it just added to the weight:
            They left reluctantly,
                        not free.

        Add one more stone
            to his burden.

Jacob, why won't you
cross the river?

Because I've come too far
I don't believe in peace anymore
I don't think
I can take it
When you've seen what I've seen—
These things can't be undone.

I still believe in peace
and I can clean
anything you
let me scrub.
But I won't
drag you
into the water.

I want to turn back.

You can't.
I won't force you forward,
but I will block your retreat.

And so the pain
sharp and to the bone
putting his hip forever out of joint;
he screams into the barren night
pinned to the ground, helpless.

This hurts me, too
I will call you Israel
because you have
wrestled with God
and won.

You call this winning?

It feels like loss
to me, too.

Set me free
    give me up
        and let me be

I can't stop
loving you.

The night is long
    and the bank is hard
        on Jacob's shoulder
            where there is no rest
        for God nor man
    on the far side of the river.

Taken from Genesis 32:6–32

In our long night of desperation, when the cloud of hope can no longer move us forward, the fire comes to claim us. We move forward again, but now we move as children fleeing a burning building. This is the time when new things are forged. It's the death, the burning up, of old things.

Jacob came away with a new name when he wrestled with God.

He also came away with a limp that lasted the rest of his life.

The pain, and the wounds, are real.

Yet the pain is necessary: the solution to our paradox does not come without a measure of death. We are, normally, a bundle of mixed motives and wants; a cup of incoherent motion, swirling, restless. We have no sure direction because we have so many competing directions inside us. And when we listen for the voice of God, when we look for guidance, we hear the swirl instead. We think we hear God make promises, and only later—much, much later, after many howls of betrayal—do we recognize those promises as made in our own voice.

Thus the gift of desolation, the burning of everything inside us, the quelling of our own restless, surging motions. The firestorm of desperation clears away our resistance to uncontrollable change. It leaves behind nothing but an empty cup, and the sound of sheer silence—not the silence of peace, but the silence of the wasteland.

Anguished, dead, bereaved silence.

The sound of God about to speak.

Martha's Endless Jar

Then the word of the LORD came to [Elijah], saying, "Go now to Zarephath, which belongs to Sidon, and live there; for I have commanded a widow there to feed you." So he set out and went to Zarephath. When he came to the gate of the town, a widow was there gathering sticks; he called to her and said, "Bring me a little water in a vessel, so that I may drink." As she was going to bring it, he called to her and said, "Bring me a morsel of bread in your hand." But she said, "As the LORD your God lives, I have nothing baked, only a handful of meal in a jar, and a little oil in a jug; I am now gathering a couple of sticks, so that I may go home and prepare it for myself and my son, that we may eat it, and die." Elijah said to her, "Do not be afraid; go and do as you have said; but first make me a little cake of it and bring it to me, and afterwards make something for yourself and your son. For thus says the LORD the God of Israel: The jar of meal will not be emptied and the jug of oil will not fail until the day that the LORD sends rain on the earth." She went and did as Elijah said, so that she as well as he and her household ate for many days. The jar of meal was not emptied, neither did the jug of oil fail, according to the word of the LORD that he spoke by Elijah.

After this the son of the woman, the mistress of the house, became ill; his illness was so severe that there was no breath left in him. She then said to Elijah, "What have you against me,

O man of God? You have come to me to bring my sin to remembrance, and to cause the death of my son!" But he said to her, "give me your son." He took him from her bosom, carried him up into the upper chamber where he was lodging, and laid him on his own bed. He cried out to the LORD, "O LORD my God, have you brought calamity even upon the widow with whom I am staying, by killing her son?" Then he stretched himself upon the child three times, and cried out to the LORD, "O LORD my God, let this child's life come into him again." The LORD listened to the voice of Elijah; the life of the child came into him again, and he revived.
{I Kings 17: 8–22}

SOMETIMES
I CAN'T TELL
THE DIFFERENCE
BETWEEN
DEATH RATTLES
AND
BIRTH PANGS.

Her love brings a jar
I can scarcely believe
Her baby's breath lies in it
     And the scent
     Of salt
        The sea
     The sound of laughter
And warm foam to end the drought

     Tall, tall waves
        Roll out like thunder
            In a tiny house too small
               For words too big to speak.

                                        And I say
                    That jar has no business filling
                                So many cups for free.

"Look inside," she laughs
        As she recedes behind the mouth
                Of her endless jar
                        Pouring out oceans,
                                planets,
                                        seagulls,
                                                stars.

When we plead for God to speak, we ask for intervention
in the normal course of things: we ask for a miracle, no
matter how humble.

That's hard to do in this world. It's hard to believe God
would have such a radical, material effect on our lives.

Do you believe in miracles? I have friends—some of
them are pastors, surprise, surprise—who filter most of
the miracle stories out of the Bible, yet still hold on to the
most astounding claim of all, that the entire universe is a
created object, made by something called "God"—and
many still believe that an executed Jewish criminal—
Jesus—came back to life on a day called Easter.

That little widow's jar, however, is just asking too much.

                "You strain out gnats,"
                said the Jewish criminal,
                "but you swallow camels."

Oh, well…
It really doesn't matter.

I mean that, with all my heart. It really doesn't matter if you believe in miracles or not. They still happen every day, with or without your permission.

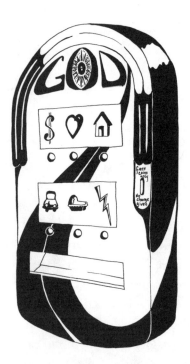

—I know, I know: there are legions of folks out there who will tell you that you have to have greater and greater faith to produce miracles. They'll tell you that you have to pray harder, you have to believe more.

For them, God operates like a giant vending machine, you see, and you have to drop the right amount of faith coins into the slot before goodies drop out the bottom—

Well, shoot. That's just another attempt to control God. It makes God depend on us, instead of the other way around.

Be suspicious of anything that makes God depend on us. There will usually be people with control problems behind it.

• • • • •

This is the testimony I have:

God has never waited for me to have great faith.

I have, in fact, crummy, low-grade faith.

I was born with a genetic disease (cystic fibrosis) that was supposed to kill me more than twenty years ago, and I thought God had done that to me on purpose. One of the first songs I wrote had these lyrics:

"I hated you from the day you were conceived.
From that point on
I had decided you'd bleed.
Now you stand before me
on your Judgement Day
I need no excuses,
I'll just throw you away."

That's the kind of faith and trust I started out with.

As I have moved through the wilderness, I have failed, fallen down, cursed and fought with God; and it has not been my richness of faith that God answered, but my poverty.

It has been an empty cup that God filled, not a full one.

God is so uncontrollable, that I cannot even gain control with my anger and unbelief. My doubt is powerless in the face of an open jar that overflows with life and breath; with the Milky Way; with oak trees, squirrels and Republicans; with DNA and the Sunday *Times*...

They all gush out of the mouth of the jar, and I cannot stop it up.

God gives constantly, recklessly, with no regard for our ability to pay for it. God *is* the bottomless jar.

The shirt you're wearing was produced by God.

This booklet in your hand was produced by God.

And that's the way the world works. We harvest what God gives, ignorantly stamp our name on it, and God never sues.

Such spendthrift, scandalous behavior on God's part! Think of the royalties being ignored.

Why, the income from cotton alone...

FAITH IS
MEMORY OF
WHAT GOD HAS
DONE.

FAITH IS AN
ACTION.

...ies and pray for...
...ate you, 45 so that you may be ch...
dren of your Father in heaven; for he
makes his sun rise on the evil and on the
good, and sends rain on the righteous
and on the unrighteous. 46 For if you...
those who love you, what re...
hav...

...T PEOPLE

NO MATTER HOW SMALL THE FAITH
IS, IT CAN BE GREAT BECAUSE OF
THE GREATNESS IN WHOM WE BELIEVE.
(– BOO BERTRAM, 9/8/92)

YOU INCREASE FAITH BY
ACTING ON MEMORY.

...oy h...
...nything, have ...y on us and help
...s." 23 Jesus said to him, "If you are
able!—All things can be done for the one
who believes." 24 Immediately the father
of the child cried out, ? "I believe; help
my unbelief!" 25 W...n Jesus saw that a...
...wd ...ame ...he re...

CRE...

	86	
	DR NUMBER	DATE

RIGHT NOW
I AM
ACTING AS
IF I
HAD FAITH,
EVEN
THOUGH
I DON'T.
SOMETIMES
ALL YOU CAN
DO IS
PRETEND.

Resurrection Passion

Now a certain man was ill, Lazarus of Bethany, the village of Mary and her sister Martha. Mary was the one who anointed the Lord with perfume and wiped his feet with her hair; her brother Lazarus was ill. So the sisters sent a message to Jesus, "Lord, he whom you love is ill." But when Jesus heard it, he said, "This illness does not lead to death; rather it is for God's glory, so that the Son of God may be glorified through it." Accordingly, though Jesus loved Martha and her sister and Lazarus, after having heard that Lazarus was ill, he stayed two days longer in the place where he was.

Then after this he said to the disciples, "Let us go to Judea again."

...When Jesus arrived, he found that Lazarus had already been in the tomb four days. ...When Martha heard that Jesus was coming, she went and met him, while Mary stayed at home. Martha said to Jesus, "Lord, if you had been here, my brother would not have died. But even now I know that God will give you whatever you ask of him." Jesus said to her, "Your brother will rise again." Martha said to him, "I know that he will rise again in the resurrection on the last day." Jesus said to her, "I am the resurrection and the life. Those who believe in me, even though they die, will live, and everyone who lives and believes in me will never die. Do you believe this?" She

said to him, "Yes, Lord, I believe that you are the Messiah, the Son of God, the one coming into the world."

When she had said this, she went back and called her sister Mary, and told her privately, "The Teacher is here and is calling for you." And when she heard it, she got up quickly and went to him. Now Jesus had not yet come to the village, but was still at the place where Martha had met him. The Jews who were with her in the house, consoling her, saw Mary get up quickly and go out. They followed her because they thought that she was going to the tomb to weep there. When Mary came where Jesus was and saw him, she knelt at his feet and said to him, "Lord, if you had been here, my brother would not have died." When Jesus saw her weeping, and the Jews who came with her also weeping, he was greatly disturbed in spirit and deeply moved. He said, "Where have you laid him?" They said to him, "Lord, come and see."

...Then Jesus, again greatly disturbed, came to the tomb. It was a cave, and a stone was lying against it. Jesus said, "Take away the stone." ...So they took away the stone. And Jesus looked upward and said, "Father, I thank you for having heard me. I knew that you always hear me, but I have said this for the sake of the crowd standing here, so that they may believe that you sent me." When he had said this, he cried with a loud voice, "Lazarus, come out!" The dead man came out, his hands and feet bound with strips of cloth, and his face wrapped in a cloth. Jesus said to them, "Unbind him, and let him go."

Many of the Jews therefore, who had come with Mary and had seen what Jesus did, believed in him.

John 11:1–7, 17, 19–34, 38–39a, 41b–45

Lazarus stands on the beach and blinks at the daylight. His hands are covered with wet sand; his expression is dazed. The sound of thunder still rings in his ears. It is the sound of fear, of the tomb. It is the stone-amplified call to freedom—Lazarus, come forth!—which yanked him out of stillness and slumber, the call he could not ignore, which now haunts him like the sound of an explosion that will not die away. It is stuck in his head: everywhere he turns he hears it.

Lazarus, come forth.

The sand is rough, grainy, even when wet. Tiny gravel. Like... sandpaper. Right.

Lazarus, come forth.

A bird sweeps across the beach with its head down, skimming for food. Its beak leaves a trail in the water. Miraculous, strange.

As miraculous as the stars overhead, already overcoming the sun, drilled like tiny holes in the azure dome. There is the morning star, there is the warrior. There, the dipper.

As strange as his body, rail-thin, fragile. People tell him that he worries them, the way he shakes in the breeze. They say he looks too delicate, ready to fall apart with the slightest bump.

Funny. That's the way the rest of the world looks to him. Fragile, precious. Like crystal. Risky to hold—put it down, you fool, you'll just drop it, and then what will you do?

Oh world, if you only knew how fragile your existence was. You don't see me shaking in the wind; you see yourself.

Lazarus, come forth.

He kneels on the shore to brace himself
against the breeze. It is invigorating and tir-
ing at the same time. If it would just turn
down a little...

His bones still ache with the welcome memory of hugs. He didn't think he would have
them again. He overindulged. Got to watch
that for a while. Spread love out again, like
butter on bread. You don't have to try to gulp
it all down like a street urchin. There's time,
time again.

Time again. God, you gave me time again. It
hurts. I can't say that without shame. I had
given up on you. In spite of all our history, in
spite of everything we'd been through
together—Lord, I should have known, I should
have held on—you saved me anyway. After I had
turned on you and declared you the enemy, you
saved me anyway.

Lazarus, come forth.

It rings in his ears. He can't get it out of his head.
Everywhere he goes, he looks dazed. It is the pain of
resurrection. He was dead, and now he's back, and
he doesn't know why.

Maybe it was
for his sister.

God knows it
wasn't for his own
sake. He deserved
nothing. He had
thrown it all away,
the foolish son. He
had given up, lost
hope.

Hope is installed deep in
the heart. It hurts to have
it put back.

Oh my dear Lord, if you think I can repay
you, put me back in the tomb. I'm out of
credit. I am bankrupt. I am—

—as dependent,
as resourceless,
as needy—
as a newborn babe.
Reborn. The cliché.

But that's the truth of it. I had
died, I had settled for the tomb
—grasped it, really, with open
arms, eager to throw away the
busyness that wore me
down—and I have seen the
sun again...

And I should be happy
right now, but all I can
feel is grief: the grief of
one who has betrayed
his deepest love, and
been forgiven.

Lazarus, come
forth.

The sand is
rough, grainy.

Where does resurrection come from? When you're looking for a new, workable direction, where do you look?
How do you listen for God's voice?

Most times, as in the case of Elijah and the widow,
God speaks through other people. Miracles are special
events. They deserve to be hand-delivered personally.

I've had many prophets enter my life, with unlikely
names. God borrowed their tongues for just a few
moments, a few magic sentences, and gave me the missing pieces. Most of the time, they were unaware of the
importance of what they said. They thought it was an off-

hand remark or an obvious observation. Sometimes they can't even remember the encounter. There were no bells ringing for them.

But bells rang when they spoke, and when I heard the words, I knew God was behind their tongues.

Other times, the missing piece has come from random digging. I have flipped through books and found the hand of God behind the words. Sometimes the book has been the Bible, but other times it's been something very unlikely, like the Meteorological Index to the Major U.S. Cities.

I suspect it's not just the book or tongue—any messenger might carry God's voice. I think the posture of the listener also has something to do with it.

Have you ever watched a heron fish?

She stands silently in the water. She is as still as the moon above her head. Sometimes she moves forward, but only after many long minutes of waiting and watching.

She knows there are fish in the sea. She knows one will come by.

She does not let the long minutes panic her, and she does not roil the waters with aimless movement. She waits, and watches. That way, when a fish comes by, she is ready. She recognizes it. She strikes.

That's how you listen for prophets.

When your own directions have burned out, when you see no more possibilities, when your soul has wrestled itself down to anguished stillness… use the stillness and the silence, even though you're anxious to end it. It is the space into which God will drop the answer.

There are fish in the sea. One will swim by.

Stay open. Listen attentively.

Pray, certainly. But stop your mouth and listen, too. God is usually very polite, and loathe to interrupt.

When you pray, ask for good listeners; then seek them out. Tell them what you're wrestling with. Ask them for reactions and random thoughts.

Don't kill minnow-sized ideas by first examining them for what's wrong. Ask what's right, first. Give them a chance to mature.

Remember the heron. Hold that image in your head, and hold on.

Fish are coming.

A LIGHT GRIND
OF TIRE
ON WEATHERED BLACKTOP
THE GRAIN OF THE ROAD
IN MY HANDS
PLEASURE IN PEBBLES
AND QUIET COASTS
DO YOU KNOW HOW
TO GLIDE?
WE HAVE TWO BIKES
AND I KNOW YOU NEVER
THOUGHT WE'D HAVE
THIS AGAIN
AND NEITHER DID I
BUT THERE IT IS
WHEN YOU STOP
PEDALING
THE ROAD TAKES YOU
GRAVITY
IS JUST A TUG ON YOUR
HANDLEBARS
AND GOD IS JUST A
DREAM
IF YOU GRIP TOO
HARD
LORD, GRANT ME STRENGTH
TO PEDAL WHEN I NEED
TO COAST WHEN I CAN
AND TO ALWAYS
STEER
LIGHTLY.

To Be Fed by Birds

The word of the LORD came to [Elijah], saying, "Go from here and turn eastward, and hide yourself by the Wadi Cherith, which is east of the Jordan. You shall drink from the wadi, and I have commanded the ravens to feed you there." So he went and did according to the word of the LORD; he went and lived by the Wadi Cherith, which is east of the Jordan. The ravens brought him bread and meat in the morning, and bread and meat in the evening; and he drank from the wadi. But after a while the wadi dried up, because there was no rain in the land.

{I Kings 17: 2–7}

I've been thinking about birds a lot lately. Can't get them off my mind; I see them everywhere here in Rockport, and they pop up in Scripture, too.

This little passage about ravens intrigues me. I've spent a lot of time sitting at the creek, myself, waiting for ravens. I recognize the scene. And I am astonished by the off-hand tone of the story, because there's incredible tension hiding behind those words.

It takes a lot to sit by a creek and wait for birds to come.

It's the moment of truth, a terrifying time when you actually behaved as if your beliefs mattered. It's the ulti-

mate gamble, really: you put your most precious things on the table and let the universe roll the dice.

Faith is always a gamble, but most of us hedge our bets. We hope we're right, but live as if we're wrong.

Yet every now and then, you hear this crazy promise... "Go sit by the wadi, and wait for ravens." And what do you do? What do you do? If you don't go, you will never know the truth, will you? And if you do go, you'll be living like a fool.

This is what we usually do: we pack a big lunch, sit by the creek for thirty minutes, and after the first stranger questions our sanity we walk sadly away with a softly muttered "Well, I tried."

Well, after that kind of tepid gamble, we start to die inside. Our failure tells us that our worst fears are true. We have proved to ourselves that the universe is a cold, heartless place, designed by an absent, shoddy, or malicious architect. And now we have to live in that universe for the rest of our lives.

What an awful punishment, doled out just for timid risk taking!

No, I think I'd rather sit by the creek and starve.

I think this is the meaning behind "Your faith has made you well." The ravens can't come unless you're there. You have to wait for ravens.

Yet God sends the ravens. You can't conjure them up by wishing hard. Elijah didn't pick any old creek, plunk himself down and summon ravens with his tremendous powers of belief.

You hear what I'm saying? The ravens were sent to the Wadi Cherith. Elijah just showed up for the meal.

But that's hard enough, isn't it?

Sometimes it's all we can do to show up for the meal.

• • • • •

Of course, speaking from personal experience, if you do continue to wait for the ravens, you will use up all the food you packed, and nothing will happen for an unbearably long time... and many people will come to you with routes to the local grocery store... and you will get hungry, and worried, and start to think you're crazy...

...and in the end, ravens won't come.

Nope, grackles or geese; seagulls, doves or whooping cranes will come instead. It will turn out that God said "bird," and you heard "raven."

A simple transmission error—happens all the time.

Elijah must have had better wiring. Me, I always hear a lot of static.

I've learned to distrust the details of my somewhat garbled calls. The times in my life that I insisted on ravens, to the point of ignoring grackles holding meat, I've lost a lot of weight.

Creek-sitting is a curious mixture of stubbornness and openness. Stubbornness to the intent of the message; openness to the details that can be disturbed by our own internal static.

But you know, the birds do come, even if they come in surprising shapes.

$$\bullet \bullet \bullet \bullet \bullet$$

Oh yeah, one more thing...

Later on, when you tell the incredible story about how you were fed by grackles, your friends and relatives will listen with the kind of expression normally reserved for children, beggars, and door-to-door salesmen. They will nod politely at all the appropriate moments, but you will have the sinking feeling that they're not really hearing you.

And when you're done, this will be their reaction:

"I thought you went out for ravens."

The world is rigged so that skeptics will never be satisfied.

But you'll remember the meat in the beak, and the look in the grackle's eyes, and you'll know. You'll know who sent it.

An Experiment in Human Creativity

Think of an entirely new animal.

It can't use parts from any other animal now existing.

It can't use anything else you've already encountered in this world. It has to be genuinely new, not just a collage of what you've already seen.

Sketch it:

I am so glad most of my prayers remain unanswered.

Coming Clean/After Words

Miracles are like drops of rain; the instant they hit the sea, they start to vanish. There is a brief moment of telltale ripples—look! Something happened here—but reality is a resilient sea that absorbs every drop, takes it into itself, and quickly erases the evidence.

The universe happened.

So what? It's always been here.

You breathe.

So what? I always have.

If it's here, there must be an explanation for it; and if there's an explanation for it, it must not be a miracle.

Thus God can produce no miracles. Everything that enters our world becomes part of our world, and therefore strangely unremarkable, commonplace.

And yet…

And yet the sea of our reality is made up of billions of tiny drops of miracle water.

God can produce no miracles—only reality.

I imagine the Creator knew that this was going to be a losing game right from the start, so I won't waste any worry about this for God's sake.

No, the real tragedy is what it means for us, for Creation.

Take a look at a new Father, already turning from the joy of his new baby to anxiety about the hospital bills.

What a shame.

Sooner or later, manna always turns into peanut butter, and more's the pity.

• • • • •

Have you ever read those long prayers in the Hebrew Bible? They have something in common, a recognizable structure.

They always start out with a long period of remembrance, where the people recall everything God has done for them. God took us out of Egypt, and across the Sea, and defeated our enemies, and brought us to water… it goes on and on, until you're about ready to fall asleep or scream. It's a very tedious custom to people from our culture.

Now you might say that this was an artifact of a mostly verbal society, preserving its history through repetition.

Or you might say that those folks knew what it took to walk into the desert.

The water-drop effect can only be defeated by people who remember the ripples. Courage to depend on God comes from an acute awareness of how one has already depended upon God.

Have you ever had a time when you thought your world was coming unglued, but you survived? Have you ever seen your worst fears pass you by?

Have you ever experienced renewal? Have you ever found your life redeemed unexplainably from a very real hell?

Or, on a broader scale, do you have talents or skills—a knack that lies dormant within you, just waiting for training so that it might bloom?

Or did you find yourself blessed with a good, caring person at a time when you most desperately needed it?

Or, even broader, do you breathe? Are there things in your life that you can take no credit for, that just seemed to drop into your lap?

There's the beginning of your list.

Faith gets easier as I get older, because my list gets longer. My heart aches for children and teenagers who are handed very adult problems with very short lists. How will they ever find hope? And my heart aches for those who were never taught to build their lists. How on earth will they ever find courage?

We don't praise God and give thanks solely for God's benefit. We praise and give thanks for our benefit. It's the only way to remember the ripples in the pond. And we remember those ripples so that we can remember the drops of miracle water: those amazing moments when we came clean from all of the cat hair and pretzel crumbs, those moments when we dropped fresh from the sky.

When you come clean, don't forget to speak the After Words.

Say them to others. Say them over and over.

That way, when you once again become sully and sore and weary of earth… you'll find it just a little easier to say goodbye to old ways and follow the cloud.

Renewal comes faster to those who walk after it.

I wish you renewal and peace.

—*Bill Williams*

Then there was the day
Wings broke out of his back
And his heart shivered
Like a loose cloak
Over the heart of a lion
He felt the grave, grave, gravity end
And the powerlessness
That fettered him
In manacles of rusty skin
Dry up and dust away
The stretch of endless Saturdays
And the laugh that would not fade away
A cheshire grin
For a winged cat, maybe,
Or maybe a fingered gull
With opposable thumbs
The better to play piano with
On strings the size of planets
All the music of the spheres
Going boom, boom, boom
And the sound across the heavens
Was the joy of his release
As he stroked across the sky
With humming wings
And eager things
To do
His companions waved goodbye
Shed a tear
And burnt an old cocoon.

*Left untitled, this was one of Bill Williams'
last poems.*

About the Illustrator

• • • • •

Martha S. Williams, Bill's wife, has been making art since she was a child. She studied art briefly in college before deciding to become a registered nurse. During her ten-year nursing career, she continued to draw and paint, providing artwork for album covers and drawings and graphics for several of Bill's video games.

The illustrations for *Manna in the Wilderness* are a continuation of the creative partnership that Martha and Bill shared throughout their walk together. The ink drawings are inspired by the trials of life and by the hope that God provides to ease the pain.

Martha currently lives and works with God and her two cats in Rockport, Texas. Her paintings and mixed-media sculptures are in private collections throughout the Midwest and Texas. Her work can be seen in Rockport at the Estelle Stair Gallery.